Pueblo Indians
of the Southwest

By Mira Bartók and
Christine Ronan

GoodYearBooks
An Imprint of ScottForesman
A Division of HarperCollins*Publishers*

W0010909

United States

The Pueblo Indians live in the southwestern states of New Mexico and Arizona.

Pueblo means "town" in Spanish.
Long ago, the Pueblo Indians' ancestors
built towns into the sides of mountains.

Sometimes they made pictures
on cliff walls and rocks.

6

Today, some Pueblo Indians live
in pueblos on high, flat mountains
called *mesas*.

There is very little rain where they live. Rain is important to farmers who need water to raise corn and other crops for food.

Some say that a rain cloud is a gift of life from the ancestor spirits.

People thank these spirits in many ways—
with ceremonies, dancing, drumming,
and by making beautiful objects.

Some call the ancestor spirits that bring rain during the growing season *kachinas*.

These dolls are models of kachinas.

The dolls help children to remember
the many kachina spirits.

Elders teach the ways of their
ancestors, keeping ancient
traditions alive.

15